The History of the Internet

The History of the Internet

Josepha Sherman

Watts LIBRARY™

Franklin Watts
A Division of Scholastic Inc.
New York • Toronto • London • Auckland • Sydney
Mexico City • New Delhi • Hong Kong
Danbury, Connecticut

Note to readers: Definitions for words in **bold** can be found in the Glossary at the back of this book.

Photographs © 2003: AP/Wide World Photos: 33 (Elise Amendola), 27 (Clint Karlsen), 35 (Seanna O'Sullivan); Archive Photos/Getty Images/Fred Prouser/Reuters: 13; BBN Technologies: 11, 17; Computer History Museum, Mountain View, CA: 5 left, 14, 16, 30, 39; Corbis Images: 48 (Michael Barley), 10 (Bettmann), cover (W. Cody), 46 (Steve Raymer), 28, 42 (Reuters NewMedia Inc.), 6; Corbis SABA/James Leynse: 41; Getty Images: 36 (Sharon Farmer/Liaison), 5 right, 44 (Oleg Nikishin), 22 (Michael Shane Smith/Liaison); MIT Museum: 12; Photo Researchers, NY/David Parker/SPL: 25; PhotoEdit: 19, 40 (Michael Newman), 2 (David Young-Wolff); Steve Walker: 21; The Image Works: 37 (Monika Graff), 49 (Steven Rubin).

The photograph on the cover shows an illustration of a computer network. The photograph opposite the title page shows students using the Internet at school.

Library of Congress Cataloging-in-Publication Data

Sherman, Josepha.
    The history of the Internet / by Josepha Sherman.
        p. cm — (Watts library)
    Summary: Explores the history of the Internet—how it was developed and refined, the people involved, and the future possibilities.
    Includes bibliographical references and index.
    ISBN 0-531-12164-X (lib. bdg.)   0-531-16211-7 (pbk.)
    1. Internet—History—Juvenile literature. [1. Internet—History.] I. Title. II. Series.
TK5105.875.I57 S5218 2003
004.67'8—dc21

                                          2002008478

Contents

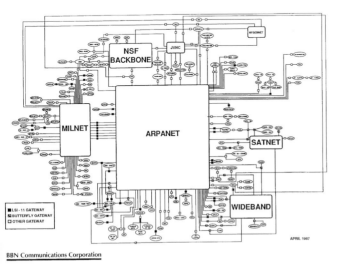

BBN Communications Corporation

Some people believe that the cables laid across the Atlantic Ocean in 1800s were the beginning of the Internet.

Chapter One

Before the Internet

It's not easy to decide when the history of the Internet actually began. Of course, there couldn't be an Internet without computers, which were invented in the second half of the twentieth century. Some people, though, claim that the Internet would never have happened at all if it hadn't been for the successful laying of the undersea transatlantic cables in 1866.

This may seem strange. The cables had nothing at all to do with computers.

They were designed to allow telegraph signals to travel from continent to continent. The success of the transatlantic cables showed that it was possible to link up two continents to allow immediate communication between them.

Maybe that idea is an ancestor of the Internet after all. But whether it is or not, nothing else happened that had anything even remotely to do with the Internet for another hundred years.

The Cold War

We might never have had the Internet in the twentieth century, or at least not have had it so quickly, if it hadn't been for a strong rivalry. This was not one taking place between teams, but between two nations. They were the two most powerful in the world, and their rivalry began in the 1940s. On one side was the United States. On the other was the Union of Soviet Socialist Republics (U.S.S.R.), which was also called the Soviet Union.

The rivalry between the two world powers was a

The Russian Revolution

The Soviet Union began with the Russian Revolution in 1917. People were tired of the demands of their czar, the Russian ruler. They overthrew the old government and set up a Communist government. Communism is an economic and political system in which the means of production and distribution of goods are controlled by the government. At the end of World War II, Russia gained control of most of the Eastern European countries and formed the U.S.S.R.

frightening thing, since both sides were well armed with nuclear weapons. If those weapons had been used, they might have ended life on Earth. But fortunately for everyone in the world, the **Cold War** stayed cold. That means that it never "heated up," or reached the danger level of all-out war. Even so, the rivalry remained intense from the late 1940s through the early 1990s. It took many forms. There were wars of words, in which each side claimed that the other was the villain. There was also a scientific and technological race to see which side would be the first into space.

Sputnik Jolts the United States

From the beginning of the Cold War, an idea had been proposed on and off by the U.S. military to create some sort of electronic network. There weren't any firm details yet about how such a network might operate. But the military people wanted a **network** that could electronically link up United States military computers in case a Soviet attack knocked out ordinary means of communications. Until the end of the 1950s, there did not seem to be any real urgency about getting such a network up and running.

Then, in 1957, the Soviets launched the first artificial **satellite**, *Sputnik I*, and everything changed. The United States was stunned. No one had dreamed that the Soviet Union was so technologically advanced. Considering the Soviets' success with the satellite, the U.S. government worried about what other technological capabilities the Soviet Union

The launch of Sputnik I *helped fuel the rivalry between the United States and the Soviet Union.*

might have. Some officials were concerned that the Soviets could block our military transmissions.

Suddenly, that first vague idea of an electronic network seemed a lot more important. Such a top secret electronic network would definitely be the way to keep the military lines of communication from being knocked out by the Soviets. In 1954, President Dwight D. Eisenhower had commissioned the Department of Defense to create the Advanced Research Projects Agency—called ARPA, for short. The parent agency, the Defense Advanced Research Projects Agency, or DARPA, still exists, and is the main research and development branch of the Department of Defense. DARPA employees think of how to use the latest technology to defend the United States. They also think of ways to ensure that enemies won't surprise the United States with their technological capabilities. ARPA's original mission was to design the first electronic network.

Getting Serious

The Department of Defense chose Dr. J. C. R. Licklider of the Massachusetts Institute of Technology (MIT) in Cambridge to run ARPA. Licklider was very excited about computers and the possibilities of linking up computers in

electronic networks. In fact, the earliest records regarding the actual birth of the Internet are a series of memos written by Licklider in August 1962. He had the idea for what he called a "Galactic Network." This would be a linked set of computers around the world through which anyone with a computer could quickly access information. And he quickly convinced everyone else at ARPA that his idea would work.

Licklider also convinced Leonard Kleinrock, another MIT scholar, who was teaching at the University of California, Los Angeles (UCLA). Kleinrock had published the first paper on what is called packet switching theory in July 1961. In computer terminology, a packet is a unit of electronic information,

This photograph shows the team that designed and deployed the ARPANET.

11

Dr. J. C. R. Licklider (right) had already been thinking of a global network when he went to work for the Department of Defense.

and packet switching means transferring packets, or packages, of information over an electronic network. This type of information transfer is a major part of **computer networking**.

The other major step in designing a working network was to find a way to get computers to talk to each other. In 1965, two university computers in California—one on the UCLA campus at Berkeley, the other at the Stanford Research Institute (SRI)—were linked up by telephone line. Kleinrock, interviewed by a reporter for *The Sacramento Bee* in 1991, described what happened next:

We set up a telephone connection between us and the guys at SRI. We typed the L and we asked on the phone, "Do you see the L?"

"Yes, we see the L" came the response.

We typed the O, and we asked, "Do you see the O?"

"Yes, we see the O."

Then we typed the G, and the system crashed.

System crashes, as anyone who uses a computer knows all too well, are a part of computer life. Despite that annoying crash, Kleinrock had just done something that would change the world of computing and of communication forever. He had created the first computer network.

Leonard Kleinrock has worked as professor of computer science at UCLA since 1963.

ARPANET Evolves Rapidly

In 1969, the Department of Defense formally commissioned, or officially ordered, the network to be set up. Since it had been developed by ARPA, it was christened ARPANET. This new computer network was quite an amazing achievement. No one, not even the scientists, could have guessed that this was only the beginning. And no one could ever have predicted what course ARPANET was going to take or how completely it was going to affect everyone's lives.

ARPANET quickly outgrew the initial idea that it was to be strictly a military network. The scientists at ARPA thought that it would become far more useful if some universities were added to the network so that the best scientific minds could help the military. Universities were also some of the few places that actually had computers at this time. The first four universities—UCLA, Stanford Research Institute, University of California, Santa Barbara, and the University of Utah—were soon added to ARPANET. By 1971 fifteen other universities and organizations, including the National Aeronautics and Space Administration (NASA), had been added.

A small number of university students soon discovered ARPANET. Now they could send messages back and forth

The ARPANET grew quickly. By December 1969, UCLA, the University of Utah, and the University of California, Santa Barbara had been added to the network.

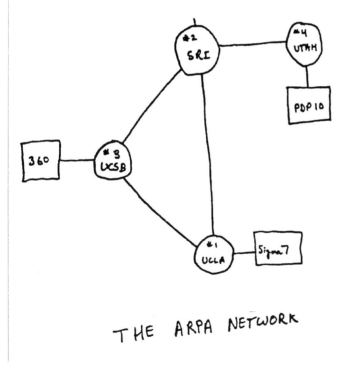

THE ARPA NETWORK

DEC 1969

4 NODES

to each other, even to friends at other universities. They could play games electronically. By 1970, the students—and a few professors as well—had turned ARPANET from its original purpose into a high-speed electronic postal system. It wasn't the form of **e-mail** we use today. All a user could do was create a text file and send it to an electronic "mailbox." The person who received the text file couldn't change it or forward it. A whole new message had to be created and sent back.

Ray Tomlinson helped create the e-mail addresses we use today.

That @ Sign

Then, in 1971, computer engineer Ray Tomlinson improved e-mail. He had already been tinkering with his own communications program. Now Tomlinson used it to modify the original design of the ARPANET e-mail system to make it simpler and more efficient. He is the one who added that "@" to all e-mail addresses. What does the symbol mean in computing? It was a symbol that Tomlinson picked at first because it was not already being used by any other computer program. Besides, as he says, "The '@' sign seemed to make sense. I used it to indicate that the user was 'at' some other **host** rather than being local." In late 1971, the first modern e-mail message was sent—from Ray Tomlinson at one computer to himself at another. The message was just a bunch of random letters. The important thing was that it worked.

Now the e-mail revolution really had begun! Everyone with access to ARPANET started sending messages back and forth. However, there were still problems to be worked out. Every computer system had to be using the right protocol, or network communications program, if they all were to stay connected. This was true in the case of international universities that wanted to be able to connect. In October 1972 the First International Conference on Computer Communications was held in Washington, D.C., to discuss just that issue. There was a public demonstration of the ARPANET, complete with forty terminals. Representatives from around the world attended.

ARPANET continued to grow with amazing speed. By 1973 it included twenty-three hosts, connecting many more universities than military sites. The year 1973 also marked the addition of the first international connection, at the University

Playing Games

Students in several universities had discovered how to use the ARPANET for fun. In the 1970s there was a weekly online student-run game based on the *Star Trek* television series. In it, the good-guy Federation battled the alien Klingons. This was a primitive game by today's standards. It was a text-only game—that is without graphics—since computer graphics were still in the future. But it was still one of the first true multiplayer computer games!

College of London, and Norway came on board soon after.

By now, many people were ignoring—or maybe had never even known—the fact that the original purpose of ARPANET had been to keep the United States military functioning in case of an attack. ARPANET had gone way beyond the original intent, although a branch reserved for the United States military remained in existence.

Changes continued to come, and come quickly. In the 1970s a system called Telnet appeared. This was a new and more efficient way of connecting to computers on the ARPANET. Telnet was originally intended to be a library system. It was designed to allow easy access to information from libraries around the country and, later, from around the world. In fact, Telnet is still used for that purpose. But since it was designed so that it could be used by almost all systems, Telnet became an excellent way to access information on the general

Telnet enabled people to find information in libraries all over the world.

Vinton Cerf is sometimes called the "Father of the Internet" because he created the architecture that allowed different types of computers in different places to communicate with each other.

Chapter Three

The Internet Explodes

In the late 1970s the electronic network began to show everyone just how useful it could be. DARPA was still doing its own research. Vinton Cerf, one of the main founders of the ARPANET, reports that in an **elaborate** test in July 1977, the information being sent went via satellite link to Norway, from Norway to London through the Atlantic Packet Satellite Network, SATNET, and back to ARPANET to the USC Information Sciences Institute.

"What we were simulating," Cerf said, "was someone in a mobile battlefield environment going across a continental network, then across an intercontinental satellite network, and then back into a wireline network to a major computing resource in national headquarters." He adds, "So the packets [of electronic information] were traveling 94,000 miles round trip, as opposed to what would have been an 800-mile round trip directly on the ARPANET. We didn't lose a **bit**!"

This was the first time such a complicated network experiment had worked so beautifully. It is really amazing that not a bit, which is the smallest particle of electronic data, was lost.

The Wild Wired World

ARPANET had by now grown wild, like a great world of linked information, but one covered with unbelievably tangled vegetation. It was a world that no one had mapped very well, or understood too well, either.

By the end of the 1970s, more people started going online. They wanted to talk to each other on all sorts of subjects, not just on the one-topic mailing lists. So, in 1979, two graduate students, Tom Truscott and Jim Ellis, invented what they called USENET, a network, independent of ARPANET, that was available to many more computer users. It was the first organized system of newsgroups, discussion groups resembling electronic bulletin boards, on the ever-expanding network. People from all over the world with computer access started getting together in these newsgroups.

URL: http://www.csu.edu.au/special/conference/...

World Wide Web:
Changing the way we work, learn and play.

A Better Address

Every computer that is linked up on the Internet has its own address—like a telephone number—which is a long string of numbers, called the Internet Protocol (IP) address. Anyone who has ever used CompuServe has seen such an address. The Domain Name System (DNS) is an improvement. Now a domain name in words, like Google.com or Nasa.gov, takes the place of numbers and is much easier for people to remember.

By 1981, ARPANET had grown to more than 213 hosts, with a new one added every twenty days. And a whole new language was springing up around it. No one knows exactly who first invented or used the word "Internet." The first use may have been in a paper by Vinton Cerf in 1974, but he never claimed to have coined the word. At any rate, people were starting to use "Internet" in place of ARPANET. Then, in his 1984 novel *Neuromancer*, science fiction author William Gibson coined the word "cyberspace." It stuck. From then on, being online was also called being in cyberspace, a place that didn't exist in reality. Or rather, cyberspace existed in what came to be called virtual reality: a place that seemed real, but wasn't.

Concerns About Security

Still more new terms sprang into existence. Some of these new words had to do with the growing concern people were having about computer security once they realized that the Internet had its spies and thieves. "Hacker" became the term for a computer expert, the type who is so fascinated by software programs that he or she has to puzzle out how they work, down to the smallest detail. A hacker may "hack" into a program, figuring out passwords and computer codes without permission, to study the program without doing any damage while in there. In fact, a hacker may then let the owner of the program know its weaknesses so that they can be corrected.

Not every computer hacker is so honest. Some people began hacking into programs not as a challenge, but to vandalize the programs or to steal secret information that could then be sold. In the mid-1980s the hackers themselves coined the term "cracker" to mean someone who breaks into a

computer to cause harm. They probably picked the word both because it rhymes with "hacker" and because criminals who break into banks are called safecrackers. The hackers did this because they were tired of the way the news media were using the word "hacker" in every case of computer crime. But the media still tend to use "hacker" in their stories.

There was good reason for concern about security, though. On November 1, 1988, the first computer virus was released. Called the Internet Worm, it disabled about six thousand

These hackers are playing a hacking game called "capture the flag" at a convention.

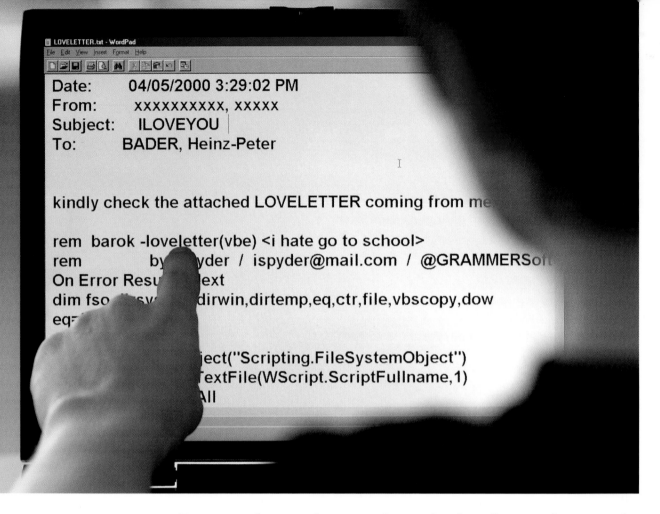

```
LOVELETTER.txt - WordPad
File Edit View Insert Format Help

Date:      04/05/2000 3:29:02 PM
From:      xxxxxxxxxx, xxxxx
Subject:   ILOVEYOU
To:        BADER, Heinz-Peter


kindly check the attached LOVELETTER coming from me

rem  barok -loveletter(vbe) <i hate go to school>
rem          by    yder  /  ispyder@mail.com  /  @GRAMMERSof
On Error Resu    ext
dim fso   sy      dirwin,dirtemp,eq,ctr,file,vbscopy,dow
eq=

             ject("Scripting.FileSystemObject")
             extFile(WScript.ScriptFullname,1)
             ll
```

A person looks at a message with the I Love You virus attached to it.

Internet hosts, fortunately only briefly. Unfortunately, though, it was only the first of literally thousands of Internet viruses, many of which are created every year. There is now a whole industry of virus-destroying software available to computer users. It is very important to install antivirus software on any computer.

Another cause for alarm came in 1989, when computer system administrator Clifford Stoll, then working for the Lawrence Berkeley Lab, caught a group of international spies—with a difference. These were **cyberspies**, spying on the United States through the Internet. Not too many people had realized that a spy could get a lot of secret information from the Net. Stoll's book about catching the cyberspies by their Internet use was called *The Cuckoo's Egg*. Although fewer than a third of the people in the United States owned computers at that time, and even fewer than those went onto the Internet, the book still became a bestseller.

No one was even using the word ARPANET anymore when it was officially decommissioned in 1990, and the true Internet was born.

The Gopher program was created by Mark McCahill and Paul Lindner at the University of Minnesota. Released in 1991, Gopher was the first "point-and-click" navigational aid to help a computer user get through the disorganized library that was the Internet. At first, McCahill and Lindner had intended Gopher to just be an aid in organizing the university's files, but they freely distributed their program on the Internet. Hundreds of people started using Gopher.

McCahill and Lindner were pleased with their invention, which certainly did make it easier to find something on the Internet. McCahill described it as "the first Internet application my mom can use."

Although Gopher could handle only text, which meant that the right commands had to be typed before anything could be found and no pictures would come with the information, it was certainly better than no organizer at all.

And what about Archie and Veronica? They were among the earliest **search engines**, programs that track down what a user is hunting for. They worked off Gopher, which meant that they returned text only. But, like Gopher and Telnet, they were perfect in the days before there were **websites** and online graphics.

Spiders and Webs

By late 1990, the Internet got an organizer it truly needed: the **World Wide Web**, or WWW (the www that starts most Internet addresses today), most often just called the Web.

There is an official description that defines the Web as "a wide-area hypermedia information retrieval initiative aiming to give universal access to a large universe of documents." That is a complicated way of saying that the Web, which is named after the image of a sticky spiderweb, helps people actually find things and bookmark them, so the pages can be found again!

Just as the idea for the Internet came not from computer users but the military, the idea for the Web also came from an unexpected place. This was the European Organization for Nuclear Research, also known as CERN. The physicists who worked there needed a way to access information quickly and

Today, Tim Berners-Lee is the director of the World Wide Web Consortium, which is dedicated to helping the Web reach its full potential.

accurately on the Internet. A computer expert named Tim Berners-Lee, working at CERN's headquarters in Switzerland, designed the first version of the World Wide Web for the physicists in 1989. Together with fellow programmer Robert Cailliau, he polished up the idea in 1990. CERN had no intention of keeping the Web to itself, and in 1991, Tim Berners-Lee made the computer code of the WorldWideWeb browser program available to the public in a newsgroup called "alt.hypertext."

Computer programmers were excited because they now had the ability to combine words, pictures, and sounds on web pages. Now not only could people find information on the Internet, but they could publish on the Internet as easily as they could use a word processor.

Websites and Online Services

It was not long after the World Wide Web became popular that ordinary people and businesses both realized they could use the Web to advertise themselves or their products. At first,

people used special computer languages, such as **Hyper Text Markup Language**, or HTML, to create websites. HTML allowed anyone who knew the codes to design a website and create the web content, the words on the site.

Then dozens of individuals and companies got into the business of web design. The companies started developing software products that would allow people to design their own websites without needing to know the HTML codes. Newer computer languages allowed website designers to create special effects such as animation and rollovers. A "rollover" is the effect seen when a cursor "rolls over" a specific spot on a website and the spot changes to a different image.

In the early 1990s, people began designing their own websites. This man created a website that provided the surf forecast for the California coast.

A Special Language

One of the earliest computer languages used by website designers is called **Java**. It was created in 1995 by James Gosling and a team of programmers at Sun Microsystems, a computer company.

Former President Bill Clinton takes a moment to visit the home page for the White House.

Governments and religious authorities wanted their own websites, too. In 1993, the United States White House opened its website. In 1994, Japan's Prime Minister went online. And in 1995, the Vatican launched its website.

Private citizens could get online more easily, too. The first of the commercial online services was CompuServe, which was founded in 1969 by Jeffey Wilkins and which offered e-mail to its clients. Unfortunately, e-mail could only be sent to and received by other CompuServe clients. The same was true at first of AOL, which began in 1985 as Quantum Computer Services and officially changed its name to America Online in 1991. By 1994, the AOL service reached one million members. There were also hundreds of smaller online bulletin boards, ranging from GEnie.com, which was originally owned by General Electric, to little services run in someone's garage or basement.

Many people turned to online service providers, such as AOL, to access the Internet.

By the 1990s most of the commercial online services offered Internet access. Before this, someone had to be part of a university or a corporation to get onto the Internet. Home computer users were shut out. Now anyone with a computer could access the Internet.

HTML

Hyper Text Markup Language (HTML) actually is not a separate language, such as French or Spanish. Instead, it is a way of adding instructions to text to tell a computer how to display them or to link to another location. In addition to learning the system of codes called tags, you should remember that an opening tag is almost always followed by a closing tag.

Here is an example:

<HTML> This is an opening HTML tag that tells the computer that what follows is to be in HTML format.

<HEAD><TITLE>MY WEB PAGE</TITLE></HEAD> "Head" and "Title" tell the computer that the text that comes between the tags is to be displayed as heading and title. The forward slash or "/" tells the computer to close the heading and title tags.

</HTML> This is the closing HTML tag.

The Great Browser War

To get to the World Wide Web, a computer user needs a **web browser**. The browser is a program that retrieves from the Web the information requested by the user, typically in the form of an HTML document. It then interprets the HTML tags and displays the formatted text. Browsers probably got their name because they allowed a user to browse through the Web as if it was a library.

In 1992 one of the first web browsers was created by Jim Clark, Marc Andreessen, and a group of student programmers at the National Center for Supercomputing Applications, NCSA, at the University of Illinois at Urbana-Champaign. Named Mosaic after the pattern, or mosaic, of information

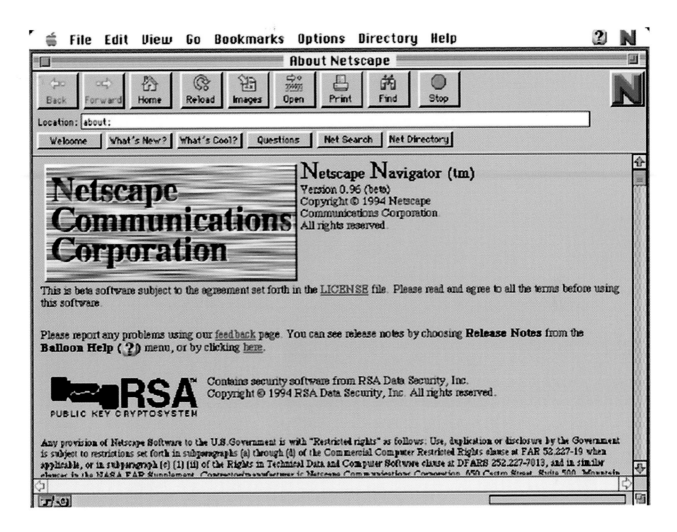

found on the Web, the browser came into use in 1993 and is still available, but not used very much.

This photograph shows what the Netscape program looked like in 1994.

Marc Andreessen saw a need for good web browsers. He and his partner, Jim Clark, founded the company Netscape soon after helping design Mosaic. They launched their new Netscape Navigator browser in 1994. It quickly became so great a success that by 1995, Netscape Navigator had become the most popular web browser.

Microsoft launched a Web browser, which competed against Netscape.

In 1995, the giant computer software company Microsoft launched its own browser, Internet Explorer. Internet Explorer, Microsoft announced, was free. So in 1998, Andreessen announced that Netscape also had become free to users.

Now what would Microsoft do? No one in the computer industry had any doubts that there was an undeclared war between Netscape and Microsoft. So fierce did the rivalry grow between the two companies that in 1999, in a case that is still going on, Microsoft had to appear in court to prove that it had not tried to destroy Netscape. As of 2002, the case had been partially resolved, but the question of whether or not Microsoft was trying to squash competition was still an issue.

Searchers and Metasearchers

The World Wide Web gives users access to the millions of websites, but that doesn't mean that a user can find what he or she is looking for without help. That help comes in the form of search engines. A search engine is a software tool that quickly goes through **databases** of the vast amounts of information on the Web and creates a list of specific sites out of all that information. For instance, anyone looking for a biography of George Washington would go to a search engine's website and type in "George Washington biography" or "Biography of George Washington," press Enter, and wait for the list to appear. This usually takes only a few seconds.

Without search engines, finding things on the Internet would be a very difficult task.

Search engines, such as Yahoo!, are available in many different languages. This person is using the Japanese version of Yahoo! in this photograph.

Two Ph.D. candidates in Engineering at Stanford University, David Filo and Jerry Yang, created what is now known as Yahoo! in 1994. Originally called "Jerry's Guide to the World Wide Web," the site was housed on their school computers and began as the creators' own lists of favorite links. The next year they transformed their hobby into an official business.

Today, more than 200 million people around the world use Yahoo! each month.

AltaVista.com was another of the first Web-based search engines. AltaVista, which means "a view from above," was created in 1995 by scientists at the Digital Equipment Corporation's Western Research Laboratory in Palo Alto, California. But close behind Altavista.com came Excite.com. The six young men who founded it—Mark Van Haren, Ryan McIntyre, Ben Lutch, Joe Kraus, Graham Spencer, and Martin Reinfried—were also in California when they came up with the idea for their search engine in 1993. But Excite.com did not actually appear until October 1995.

Dozens of search engines appeared from 1995 to 1998. There are too many to list them all here. Many of these search engines, like Lycos.com and Hotbot.com, soon merged, and others simply failed. One of the more recent successful search engines is Google.com, which was founded in 1998 by Larry Page and Sergey Brin, two Stanford University students working on their Ph.D. degrees.

Meanwhile, programs called metasearchers were also developed. These programs are not search engines. Instead, they hunt through several search engines at one time. The purpose was to make a search faster and more efficient. An example of a metasearch engine is Dogpile.com.

People around the world are using the Internet.

Chapter Five

The Internet Today

By the beginning of the new **millennium**, the Internet had become a familiar word to practically everyone in the world. Literally almost every nation in the world was online, from Andorra to Zaire. Millions of people continue to log on every hour, chatting with each other, playing games, hearing music from around the world, and downloading information. Politicians today casually talk about the Internet as the **information superhighway**.

Connecting the World

So far, there seem to be very few corners of the world where that superhighway can't reach. Wherever there is electricity, there seems to be a way for people to reach the outside world. There have been messages to the rest of humanity from war-torn Bosnia or flood-ravaged Bangladesh. In fact, the only

Shopping on the Web

In 1994, Pizza Hut really started something when it accepted an order for a mushroom, pepperoni, and extra cheese pizza over the Internet. People quickly realized that shopping over the Internet was possible. In less than five years, there were literally hundreds of online stores. A computer user could buy anything from books to antiques or bid in auctions at any hour of the day. Many of the sites went out of business, just as is true of any new store, but others thrived. Some of the more successful online sites include Amazon.com and eBay.com.

limitation on the Internet seems to be language. Right now, English-speakers are in luck: about 80 percent of websites are in English, or have an English translation.

However, even if the worldwide use of the Internet is still limited by language, thanks to local forms of the Internet, there are now some truly wonderful ways for people in poor nations to exchange data and get help. Recently, people in the very poor Indian district of Dhar, farmers who earn less than $300 a year, became linked to the Indian-based branch of the Internet thanks to a local program called Gyandoot.

Now the farmers of Dhar can use the Internet to check the best places to sell their crops or cows and find the best prices for supplies. Before, a trip to check family or farm records meant a long, tiring journey. Now the farmers can get in touch with their government with a few clicks of a mouse. They can also get money due to them without having to wait for days or even months. Dhar has very little reliable electricity, but the farmers are experimenting with solar power to give them electricity—and steady Internet access.

Dangers and Benefits

It's also true that there are increasing problems with security and privacy on the Internet. You can find out almost anything about anybody there if you know where to look. Online identity theft is becoming a very real issue, particularly in the case of terrorists who might want to pretend to be ordinary citizens.

The advantages of the Internet continue to far outweigh

It's important to take steps to protect your identity and financial information, whether you are shopping online or visiting a chat room.

any of the disadvantages. The Internet allows people to connect and share ideas and information regardless of where they are in world. In fact, some people no longer work in offices, but use the Internet to **telecommute** to work instead. This is a great opportunity for anyone who lives too far away to make an easy daily journey, has small children and no access to day care, or who is physically disabled and unable to travel.

The Internet is also changing the lives of students by putting more information at their fingertips. Schools have

Music Comes to the Web

The computers of the 1980s did have sound systems, but these were very primitive. They could beep tunes, but that was about it. But that situation changed for the better very quickly. By the 1990s, all computers came with sound systems. There were separate speaker attachments and stereo sound.

In 1992, the first audio and video broadcasts took place over the Net, at a site called the "M-Bone." By 1995, the system had so improved that the Rolling Stones were able to broadcast their Voodoo Lounge tour over the M-Bone.

Today, it's no longer unusual to listen to worldwide radio broadcasts over the Net, or to hear live talk shows. Even world-famous orchestras like the New York Philharmonic think nothing of broadcasting their live concerts over the Internet.

begun using the Internet as a link to a wealth of information, more than could be held in even the biggest library. This helps schools that have small budgets for buying new books give their students access to the most up-to-date information for reports and other projects.

The Internet allows you to see things you might never get a chance to in real life. You can see great works of art in museums and art galleries that are online. Some of them are now making use of three-dimensional imagery that makes images of statues seem almost like the real thing.

Building a New World

The Internet enables people to create communities and cross borders like never before. Doctors around the world use the Internet to hold medical consultations and instantly exchange vital medical information with each other. People can watch the building of the International Space Station live online and see other news around the world even as it happens. And it is even possible to stay connected to people in space. Today, astronauts can send and receive e-mail.

This worldwide sharing is something that has never happened before in the known history of the world. But what does it mean for us all? What is this sudden flood of information and free conversation going to mean to the world's people? No one can say. But whatever forms the Internet may take, one thing seems certain: The Internet is building a brand-new world for us, one that is completely without borders.

Timeline

1866	The first transatlantic cables are successfully laid.
1954	The United States forms the Advanced Research Projects Agency, ARPA.
1957	U.S.S.R. launches *Sputnik I*, the first artificial earth satellite.
1961	Leonard Kleinrock publishes the first paper on packet-switching theory.
1962	J. C. R. Licklider publishes the first paper on the "Galactic Network" concept.
1965	The first linking of two computers is successful.
1966–1968	ARPANET is planned.
1969	ARPANET is commissioned by the Department of Defense.
1970s	Telnet is begun.
1971	Ray Tomlinson invents an e-mail program.
1972	Ray Tomlinson's e-mail program is a hit with ARPANET. He introduces the @ sign. International Conference on Computer Communications (ICCC) takes place in Washington, D.C.
1973	First international connections to the ARPANET take place as the University College of London, England, links up.
1975	First ARPANET mailing list, MsgGroup, is created by Steve Walker. *Shockwave Rider* by John Brunner is published.
1976	Queen Elizabeth II sends the first royal e-mail.

1984	*Neuromancer*, by William Gibson, is published.
1988	The Internet Worm, the first computer virus, hits the Internet on November 1.
1989	*Cuckoo's Egg* by Clifford Stoll is published.
1990	ARPANET officially ends, and the Internet begins.
1991	Gopher is created by Paul Lindner and Mark P. McCahill of the University of Minnesota. The World Wide Web (WWW) is made available to the public by Tim Berners-Lee.
1992	Veronica, a Gopher search tool, is released by the University of Nevada.
1993	The United States White House opens its website.
1994	The first online shops appear. Pizza Hut takes its first online order. Online dial-up systems such as CompuServe, America Online, and Prodigy, begin to provide Internet access.
1995	The first search engines appear.
1996	The browser war begins between Netscape and Microsoft.
1998	E-commerce and e-auction sites become popular on the Internet.
1999	Saudi Arabia allows Internet access.

Glossary

bit—the smallest piece of electronic data

Cold War—the fierce rivalry between the United States and the Soviet Union between the 1940s and 1990s

computer networking—linking up a group of computers electronically

cyberspy—a person who uses the Internet to spy on other people

data—information

database—a collection of information that is arranged so that it can be easily searched

elaborate—complicated or detailed

e-mail—a message sent electronically

To Find Out More

Books

Berry, Charles W. and William H. Hawn, Jr. *Computer and Internet Dictionary for Ages 9 to 99*. Hauppauge, NY: Barron's Educational Series, Inc., 2000.

Bingham, Jane, Fiona Chandler, and Sam Taplin. *Internet-Linked Encyclopedia of World History*. London: Usborne Publishers Ltd, 2001.

Staff, Grolier Educational. *Visual Science Encyclopedia: Vol. 10: Computers and the Internet*. Danbury, CT: Grolier, 2001.

Wolinsky, Art. *The History of the Internet and the World Wide Web*. Berkeley Heights, NJ: Enslow Publishers, Inc., 1999.

Organizations and Online Sites

Birth of the Internet
http://smithsonian.yahoo.com/birthoftheinternet.html
Created by the National Museum of American History and Yahoo, this online site offers information on people, companies, and major events related to the development of the Internet and the World Wide Web.

History of Internet and WWW: The Roads and Crossroads of Internet History
http://www.netvalley.com/intval.html
This online site provides information on the history of the Internet and links to other sites on the subject.

Internet Society
http://www.isoc.org/internet/history/
This organization's Internet Histories page offers links to many sites containing historical information on the Internet.

A Little History of the World Wide Web
http://www.w3.org/History
This online site contains a timeline of the World Wide Web with links to more information.

Nerds 2.0.1

http://www.pbs.org/opb/nerds2.0.1/

This is the online site for the Public Broadcasting Service series Nerds 2.0.1, which looks at the history of the Internet. At the site, visitors can find a glossary, timeline, and biographical information on some of the key figures.

A Note on Sources

Both Internet sites and printed books were of great use in the writing of this book. Among the most valuable of the numerous Internet sites about the history of the Internet were the Internet Society's site and the History of the Internet and WWW: The Roads and Crossroads of Internet History site. Both of these sites are listed in the To Find Out More section. I also found World Wide Web inventor Tim Berners-Lee's online site invaluable.

Useful books included the comprehensive *Internet-Linked Encyclopedia of World History* by Jane Bingham, Fiona Chandler, and Sam Taplin, and Art Wolinsky's *The History of the Internet and the World Wide Web*.

—*Josepha Sherman*

Index

Numbers in *italics* indicate illustrations.

Cyberspies, 28–29

DARPA (Defense Advanced
    Research Projects
    Agency), 10, 23
DNS (Domain Name Sys-
    tem), 25
Dogpile.com metasearch
    engine, 43

E-mail, 17–18, 21, 37, 50
Eisenhower, Dwight D., 10
Elizabeth II, Queen of Eng-
    land, 21
Ellis, Jim, 24
European Organization for
    Nuclear Research
    (CERN), 33–34
Excite.com search engine, 43

Filo, David, 42
First International Confer-
    ence on Computer
    Communications, 18

Gibson, William, 26
Google.com search engine,
    43
Gopher program, 31–32
Gosling, James, 36

Gyandoot program, 47

"Hackers," 26, *27*
Hosts, 17, 18, 25, 27
Hotbot.com search engine,
    43
HTML (Hypertext Markup
    Language), 35, 38

Information Sciences Insti-
    tute, 23
International connections,
    18–19
Internet Explorer, 40, *40*
Internet Worm, 27
IP (Internet Protocol)
    addresses, 25

Java, 36

Kleinrock, Leonard, 11,
    12–13, *12*
Kraus, Joe, 43

Library systems, 19, *19*
Licklider, J. C. R., 10–11, *12*
Lindner, Paul, 32
Linux-based operating sys-
    tems, 20
Lycos.com search engine, 43

About the Author

Josepha Sherman is an author, editor, and professional folklorist. For Franklin Watts, she has written two other Watts Library titles, *Internet Safety* and *The History of the Personal Computer*. She has also written several biographies on important people in technology, including *Bill Gates: Computer King*, *Jeff Bezos*, and *Jerry Lang and David Philo: Chief Yahoos*. She has authored more than forty novels, including fantasy and science fiction.